A
COLUMBINE SURVIVOR'S STORY

By
Marjorie Lindholm
And
Peggy Lindholm, L.P.C., CAC II

Regenold Publishing
Littleton, Colorado

Published by:
Regenold Publishing Company
PO Box 621967
Littleton, Colorado 80162-1967

Cover Design by: Budget Book Design

Library of Congress Control Number: 2005933389

Printed in the United States of America

Publisher's Cataloging-In-Publication Data
(Prepared by The Donohue Group, Inc.)

Lindholm, Marjorie.
    A Columbine survivor's story / by Marjorie
Lindholm and Peggy Lindholm.--1st ed.--

      p. ; cm.
    ·ISBN: 0-9773085-0-2

1. Columbine High School (Littleton, Colo.)--
Students--Biography. 2. Columbine High School
(Littleton, Colo.)--Students--Juvenile literature.
3. School shootings--Colorado--Littleton--Personal
narratives. I. Lindholm, Peggy. II. Title.

LB3013.33.C6 L56 2005
373.788/82/092   2005933389

Acknowledgement

We'd like to thank our family and friends for their love and support throughout the years.

Disclaimer:

This book is based on the author's memories regarding actual experiences in her life. The opinions expressed within this work are that of the author(s), and are not necessarily the opinions of the publisher or any other person(s) mentioned within the book.

The names and likenesses of several people have been changed to protect their privacy.

This Book is Dedicated to:

The many people whose lives were forever changed at
Columbine High School on
April 20, 1999
Especially those who were injured or killed
And their loved ones

"May God Bless Us All"

Table of Contents:

PREFACE

I'm a survivor. That's what they say; you know, everyone who knows my past and has seen me struggle, felt my disappointment. I'm a survivor, as if that sums it up. Sometimes I feel like my life changed in an instant, and I went from the girl that could not be explained in volumes, to a woman who can be explained in a single word.

When I was a little girl, and things would go wrong, my mother would say, "Margie, if life deals you lemons, make lemonade." Then she'd say, "You're extra sweet; you can make pink lemonade."

It always made me feel better. Sometimes, my mom would call me her pink lemonade girl, because she could count on me to make the best of a bad situation; I always bounced back, until April 20, 1999.

I was in the Science Room at Columbine High School the day of the world famous shootings. I entered the building on that Tuesday morning as a normal girl with big plans, a fast moving freight train heading to glamorous destinations. By the end of that day, I was a different person, and the world never looked the same again.

CHAPTER 1
The Good Life

My name is Marjorie. I'm originally from Aurora, Colorado, but my family moved to Boise, Idaho when I was barely three. My earliest memories are of Idaho. I had a wonderful childhood with excellent parents. Even the story of their courtship was romantic.

My dad's name is Frank. When he met my mother, he was a widower with a young daughter. My mother worked at the daycare that his daughter, my older sister, Joyce, attended. Joyce was five years old and enrolled in the kindergarten. My mom was the teacher in the baby room and didn't work with Joyce, but Dad was a very handsome man. He was tall and rugged with dark blond hair and bright blue eyes. He had a hearty laugh and was always in a good mood.

My mother was a beautiful woman, five feet six inches tall with blond hair and blue eyes. She was very thin with a small frame. He caught a glimpse of her one day and looked for her every chance after that. They claimed it was love at first sight, and they were married within months. They were a striking couple, even while I was growing up, but they never looked quite like the couple they described.

My mother hadn't changed much at all. She was still small and blond; everybody said I had the prettiest mom around, but my dad didn't resemble the guy in the story at all. It's hard to believe he ever did, but they had pictures to prove it. For as long as I can remember, my dad had a laundry list of health problems. Sometimes he couldn't get out of bed for days, weeks even. His health had gotten so bad, that he had several different surgeries performed when I was very young. I always felt bad about that; I felt sorry for him, but he never complained.

My mother was already 27 years old when they met, so waiting to have a child wasn't even a consideration. I was born just a year after they were married. My sister, Sarah, came along about a year and a half later, and my baby brother, David, was born a few months before I turned three.

Joyce and I were never very close. She was almost seven years old by the time I was born, so we didn't have a lot in common, but Sarah and I were inseparable. My parents bought us everything alike; we even dressed alike. It was almost as if we were twins, best friends for as long as I can remember. Sometimes, I thought she was difficult. Sarah was always getting herself into trouble, and I had to get her out. She had a big mouth and a little body, not a good combination, but I love her, and she is an unbelievably fun person to be around.

David is much younger than me; he always seemed like a little kid when I was growing up. We were always close, but he's a boy, and he had his own friends. We played video games together, but that was about it. He hung out with his friends, or my mom, or my dad.

When David was little, my dad would take him along on his business calls. My dad was a self employed painter, and he always liked David around. People said that no man ever wanted a son more than my dad. The family wasn't complete until David arrived.

They had their guy stuff. They collected coins on a regular basis. They spent hundreds of hours searching for coins and deciding which ones they needed. David looked more like our dad than the rest of us. They were so cute together, back then.

While we lived in Idaho, I didn't feel responsible for my younger brother and sister. My dad was our protector, always. I can remember when Sarah was about 5 or 6 years old. She was always small for her age, and she always had a million friends. She had a little playhouse made of heavy plastic that looked like a tiny log cabin. On one particular night, Sarah had a sleep over, and she and her friends decided they wanted to sleep outside, in the log cabin.

Sarah was so excited. She asked my dad if he wanted to join them. I remember he looked shocked, but then he looked honored, like he couldn't believe those tiny little girls wanted him to join in the fun. Then Sarah explained that he would not be joining them; she needed him for protection. They wanted him to sleep on the ground, outside the door to the playhouse, so no wild animals could attack them. The amazing part of that story is that my father actually did it, and he never complained. He was that kind of person. As we got older, we'd have sleepovers and invite our friends to sleep on the trampoline outside. Again, our dad would sleep on the ground, off by himself, as our protector. No girl could have asked for more.

Boise has a small town feeling. We lived in the same neighborhood for more than eight years, and it seemed like we knew everyone. There was no fear about our safety. The people are very religious, mostly Mormons, and you feel safe. Nobody was scared, ever. I can remember sneaking out during sleepovers to toilet paper a friend's house. It could be 2:00 in the morning and the worst thing that could happen was getting caught. Even then, the punishment was cleaning up the mess we caused. It was always a safe place to live, and, if it is the only place you've ever known, you take that for granted. We never even heard about crime or violence happening in our world. It seemed like a foreign concept, something that only happened to people far away from us.

More than anything, I wanted to be a cheerleader. We didn't have any relatives close by, but my mother's best friend, Tina, was like an aunt to us. She had three sons and one daughter. Her oldest son was about ten years older than me and away at college. He was an excellent athlete. When he was home, he'd spend hours helping me work on my cheerleading routines, like a big brother.

Often, Tina's daughter would baby-sit for us. There were two younger boys. One of them was about my age, and the other was David's age. They were the closest thing to family that we had in Idaho, like two boy cousins. It never felt like we were alone in the world, because we had family close by, even if they weren't blood relatives.

I always had a best friend from school. Monica was my very best friend from the time I was in the third grade. We did everything together. We got involved in gymnastics at the same time and practiced constantly. We made up little dances and even got trampolines at the same time. Her mom was like my mom, and my mom was like hers. I think we slept at each other's houses every weekend for four years. I can't imagine a better way to grow up.

In seventh grade, we started Fairmont Junior High. The junior high in Boise was seventh, eighth and ninth grades, while high school was tenth, eleventh, and twelfth. Every sport available to the high school kids was available to us. Monica and I were cheerleaders and very popular. Around seventh grade, our friendship started to cool off. Monica's parents divorced and she moved away to a different area and a different school.

About that time, Carla became my best friend. I remember a boy named Paul. I think he was probably the first boy I ever really liked. Carla and I decided to toilet paper his house one night. We did that stuff back then, everybody did. Anyway, I was sleeping over at her house on a Friday night, and we snuck out around 2:00 in the morning. We giggled the whole way to his house, planning our attack and marveling at how funny it would be when he discovered the prank the next morning. We pictured his parents making him clean it up, and him wondering who could have done it.

As soon as we stepped into the front yard, Paul and one of his friends raced from behind the bushes. They had raw eggs, ketchup, and mustard, and they chased us down the street throwing the eggs and squirting the condiments. I don't think I ever laughed so hard about anything. We laughed all the time. We knew everybody in our little area, and they knew us. In ninth grade, I was actually the head cheerleader. I was the number one athlete at school and voted the second most popular girl.

We had two cats for more than ten years, Rusty and Sugar. Sarah is a cat person. She loves animals of all kinds, but she is a cat person. Our cats were outside cats, and they always ran free. Everybody's cats ran free. We never worried that somebody would want to hurt them, or that they wouldn't be coming home. We never heard about things like that happening around us.

Most of my friends had trampolines or small above ground swimming pools. We played on each other's tramps and swam in each other's pools. That's small town life. You get used to that. You think everyone lives that way.

From the outside, we looked like the perfect family, and I thought we really were. My parents did everything for us. We ate dinners as a family and did fun activities together. Every Sunday was family day. We went to the movies and out to eat as a family. Every year, we went to the Western Idaho Fair.

That was a big family project. We'd plan a little business and work on it for weeks before the fair. My dad would rent a space, and we'd have a little booth. My parents would work at the booth while the rest of us enjoyed the fair. It had everything a person could imagine. The fair sold all day ride passes and would issue a bracelet to signal you'd bought that pass. My parents always bought us those bracelets. For ten days, we rode the rides and ate cotton candy and caramel apples. We played the games and watched the magic shows and puppet theaters. All the while, our parents worked their carnival booth, and we always ate lunch together. My dad said that we spent more money than we could ever make at that fair, but he said it with a laugh. He loved it too.

One year, we sold home made jewelry, and the next, we laminated driver's licenses or pictures for people. There was a year when my dad bought a little scanner. My parents would scan a person's hand, and the machine would print out a picture of the hand and the person's fortune, like a little palm reader. My dad used to say that my mom could bring in customers just by looking at them. They made a great team. We'd see neighbors and friends; everybody went to the fair. I looked forward to that all year.

We were extremely close; my parents spent their lives on us, and we thrived on that. We weren't rich. My father is a veteran from the Vietnam War. He was wounded by gunshots and shrapnel during his service and had several physical disabilities. Sometimes he worked as a painter, but some of the time, he couldn't work.

Chapter 2
The Perfect Family

My dad paid for every lesson I ever wanted to take. Sometimes it seemed like I took 200 lessons a month. I was in tap, ballet, jazz, cheerleading, gymnastics, basketball, volleyball, softball, track, tennis, soccer, and swimming. I took Karate lessons, and I play the violin and the electronic keyboard. All of that cost a fortune to start, let alone the cost of the supplies needed to succeed in them. He never said no. It wasn't even a question.

I didn't stick with everything, but that wasn't a problem. My parents encouraged us to try anything, to reach for the stars. My life revolved around dance, cheerleading, and gymnastics. I went to at least three lessons a week for eight years. It was a constant drain on the family finances, but my dad never complained. He never even mentioned it. Instead of complaining, he built me a balance beam and uneven bars; he bought me a trampoline and marveled at my skill. We actually had duck tape running the entire length of the family room floor for over a year, so that I could practice the balance beam without fear of being hurt.

I remember when my dad built me the balance beam and uneven bars. I was probably in the fifth grade, and I didn't understand business at all. I had $300 in my savings account, and we figured that the cost of supplies would be $400. My dad said that if I wanted the equipment, I could hire him to build it, and we would split the cost of the supplies. He told me that labor charges were usually about $100.

It wasn't until after the job was complete, and he presented me with a bill for half of the supplies, that he realized I didn't understand what he meant. I thought he owed $100 more than me, because I gave him a job.

My mother kept saying, "Margie, he works for you."

Then I'd say, "I know, because I GAVE him a job. Labor is $100."

In the end, we split the cost of supplies, and he paid me $100, because I gave him a job. He was like that, my hero.

My mother supported me in every whim. She spent her life giving rides for my siblings and me; she spent her time sitting at practices, watching her children. She was my biggest fan. My mom and I went out to eat every day after school or before my lessons for as long as I can remember. It seemed like they spent their lives supporting my dreams and telling me to aim for the stars.

Sarah, David, and I were close. I taught Sarah dance, gymnastics, and cheerleading. I played video games with David. They looked up to me.

My dad was the perfect father. He had something special going on with each of us, one on one time that only we did together. My dad and I were constantly getting into crazy stuff; we always had a project. We entered every sweepstakes that came in the mail and always said that we were going to win a million dollars. That went on for years.

Once, he bought an ice cream machine. He'd actually sit on the corner with me, and we'd sell ice cream. Mostly, we ate the ice cream. After that, we dove into math.

He was always playing math games with me; it's my specialty. He bought this special program, and we learned how to turn sounds into numbers. It was a language of math. We both learned the math language and spoke in numbers. It was our secret language. Not many dads would ever do that; not many dads could do that, but mine did.

When I wanted to be a gymnast in the Olympics, my dad supported that. When I decided I'd rather be a cheerleader, my dad supported me. During junior high, I decided I wanted to be a plastic surgeon when I grew up. I excelled in math and science; I excelled in all my classes. I loved learning about surgeries and watching them on television. When I told my dad I wanted to be a doctor, he thought it was a great idea, and he bought me books and watched the Discovery Channel with me. He was like that with each one of us. Now that I'm older, I realize how rare that is. Back then, I took it for granted.

My mom was the same. She took us everywhere and got into little projects with each of us. She loved crafts and sewing. We sewed all our own Halloween costumes. It was so much fun. She was very into the holidays. We always went to Shopco and bought buttons, earrings, shirts, stickers, and decorations for every holiday.

She made everything exciting and so much fun. I loved when she made gingerbread cookies for my dad; they were his favorite. She always let us frost them, and it was such a mess. She put sprinkles on healthy food to make us think it was a treat. I loved hanging out with my mom. She was my best friend, and all my other friends knew it. When my friends came over, we all hung out with her. I still do that; I never grew out of it.

When you grow up like that, you feel invincible, like every accomplishment is yours, like no hurdle is too high. I appreciated my parents, but the glory was mine. I pictured myself as a force, a speeding freight train that would not stop short of my goals. I was determined and sure that nothing could stop me. I was going to be a doctor, a plastic surgeon. I couldn't imagine being anything but successful and happy; the possibilities were limitless. That was then.

When I was in the seventh grade, my father moved back to Colorado while the rest of the family stayed in Idaho. Denver offered more opportunity for him, and he wanted to attend college in Colorado to study the law. My mother stayed in Boise with the children. We made every effort to sell the house, so that we could join him, but that dragged on and on.

He visited every month and called home most nights. Sarah and I flew to Denver once, just the two of us, while my mom and David stayed behind. My dad had an apartment in Aurora. He had very nice furniture and expensive electronics and computers. We ate out almost every meal and rented movies every night.

On that visit, we spent a few days with my Aunt Theresa in Littleton. She is my mother's sister and best friend. They've always been best friends, and even when we lived in Idaho, they talked at least once a week. Before we moved to Idaho, they were inseparable. I don't really remember those times firsthand. I have a little rag doll called my Aunt Theresa doll. My mom has told the story so many times, it almost seems like a real memory, but I was just too young.

When I was very little, my parents worked the family business. After my mother had David, it was very hard for her to take all three children along, so my parents hired a babysitter. I didn't like her to leave me behind, and it broke her heart when I cried, so she bought a little rag doll with just a few strands of yellow yarn for hair. She named the doll Mommy. She told me that when she couldn't be there, the Mommy doll would take her place, and I was safe.

Well, Aunt Theresa was at our house all the time and saw the doll. The next thing my mom knew, Aunt Theresa had bought a more elaborate rag doll with longer hair, and she named it Theresa. A short time later, somebody, either my mother or my father, bought a little rag doll of Ziggy, the cartoon character, and he became my Daddy doll. I don't actually remember getting those three dolls, but I kept them close all through the years. I still have them, so even though I hadn't seen much of Aunt Theresa, I had her doll, and we had a bond.

Chapter 3
Journey to Columbine

By summer of 1998, my dad had been living in Colorado for two years, and our house in Boise remained unsold. My parents were concerned that it would be a mistake to wait any longer before moving the family to Colorado. The new school year would be starting soon, and they didn't want us to be switching schools in the middle of the year, so in July of 1998, my mom, Sarah, David, and I joined my dad. Joyce stayed behind in Idaho; she was older and had a good job and a steady boyfriend.

We spent those first days traveling between Aurora and Littleton, until we decided to stay with my Aunt Theresa's family. My mother wanted to live in Littleton. Besides my Aunt Theresa, she had a sister, Joanne, and a brother, Jerry, who lived in the very same area. They all spoke highly of the school system and the opportunities in education and athletics. My mother and Aunt Theresa set about finding a rental house before the school year started.

My parents decided the house had to have at least four bedrooms, 2 bathrooms and a basement. My aunt's neighborhood and many of the surrounding neighborhoods had covenants, rules the residents had to live by. My dad had to be able to park his construction trailer on the street, so there could be no covenants in any neighborhood in which we would live.

At that time, real estate in the Denver area was in great demand, and the prices seemed to be rising by the day. Our family home hadn't sold yet. We needed to find a rental property at a reasonable rate before the school year started, and we wanted to live close to my mom's family. It seemed almost impossible. They combed the paper and called many realtors before finding a house that met every condition and still fell within our budget. I was so excited, until I saw it.

It was a big house in a nice neighborhood, about five minutes from my aunt's house. It was close to Ken Caryl Middle School, where Sarah and David would be enrolled. It was right down the street from Columbine, my new school. The house had a huge yard and lots of room for my dad's trailer. From the outside, it seemed perfect. Then we walked inside.

It was awful. For some reason, there was very little sunlight, and the entire house was gloomy. The cabinets and trim were the darkest wood. The carpet was a deep brown and smelled of dog urine. The kitchen counters had stains and burn marks, and the appliances were old and dirty. The basement was dank and unfinished. The price was ridiculous.

Our home in Boise had been perfect, beautifully maintained. The rooms were bright and spacious. It had a homey feel and always put me at ease. There was no way I thought we could ever live in that rental; it was disgusting, but there wasn't any choice. It was all they could find. We had to make the best of it.

The days that followed were frenzied. There was barely two weeks before school was to start, and we hadn't even settled in or gotten our belongings from Idaho. My mother went about enrolling us in the local schools during the day, while she worked feverishly to clean the rental house at night. The Jefferson County School District required immunizations that my old school didn't, and we had to get those shots before they would permit us to enroll. There were a million and one things to do, and we set about checking each one off the list and proceeding to the next. We were so excited.

Columbine is a beautiful school with two levels and windows everywhere. It sits adjacent to Clement Park, acres of green grass and tall trees. There are baseball diamonds and soccer fields, playgrounds, and a big lake surrounded by a walking track. The western view is comprised of the prettiest mountains I've ever seen, like a picture post card. I fell in love with that view and felt so lucky to be a part of it.

I wasn't nervous about starting Columbine. It's a big school, but my junior high in Boise was every bit as big as Columbine. The high school I was planning to attend was probably twice the size of Columbine, so I wasn't that intimidated. In Idaho, we didn't have many new kids. When we did, they were usually welcomed and popular. I guess that's why I never even thought about making friends once we got to Colorado.

Columbine wasn't like that at all; it wasn't welcoming at all. Mostly, people kept their distance. I wasn't used to that, and I wasn't prepared for that. At first, I didn't have anybody to eat lunch with, and that was my biggest concern. One day, a girl named Ellen approached me and was very friendly. She was popular and a cheerleader. Ellen was a small girl with a big personality, and she reminded me of my sister, Sarah. Ellen called me all the time and introduced me to all her friends. They weren't very accepting, but at least I knew people. That was a Godsend, and I needed it.

Chapter 4
Calm Before the Storm

I was very outgoing and friendly, back then. I talked to all my teachers, especially about cheerleading. Tryouts for cheerleading were in early April. Ellen, Sarah, and I practiced all the time. I was looking forward to getting back on track, and my sister, Sarah, dreamed of making the freshman squad. Sarah and I had been taking gymnastic lessons a couple of times a week, but it was a drain on the family finances. Often, my mother was scraping together money for school supplies and clothes, but my parents promised me there would be no problem with the costs involved with cheerleading.

When the new team was announced, and my name was included, I was thrilled. Sarah didn't make the squad that year, and she was devastated. Sarah made the cheerleading team in Idaho before our move to Colorado. Had we stayed there, she would have already been a cheerleader. I felt like I couldn't show my enthusiasm at home as much as I would have liked, but it was exciting.

Almost immediately after forming the squad, the cheerleading activities went into high gear with meetings and the like. I remember April 19, 1999. It was a wonderful day. Even though it was a Monday, school flew by, and I went to a cheerleading meeting that evening. At that meeting, everything seemed to fall into place.

My closest friends knew I'd had a crush on one particular boy, Troy, for most of the school year. We had lunch at the same time, sixth period, and I looked forward to seeing him everyday. He was a football star, and I'd never even met him. I didn't think he even knew who I was, but after the cheerleading meeting, Ellen couldn't wait to tell me the rumor that Troy liked me.

I went home that night and spent what seemed like hours picking out the perfect outfit for the next day. I settled on a blue tank top and black pants. I could barely sleep thinking how lucky I was. I could hardly wait for morning.

I woke up long before the alarm sounded. I fixed my hair ten different ways before putting it up with purple butterfly clips. I eyed the outfit I had laid out the previous evening, wondering how I was going get past my father wearing that top. In those days, my father would park himself at the kitchen table in the morning, and I had to walk past him on my way out the door. He never had many rules, but when it came to the way we dressed, my father was a conservative man. He was sure every guy on the planet was after his daughters, and it was his job to keep them at bay. Normally, I liked that; it made me feel important to him, but on this very special day, it was the biggest obstacle I could imagine. I knew my mother would understand.

There was a used uniform sale scheduled for that afternoon. At that sale, cheerleaders could sell their old uniforms to the incoming squad. They were also going to have information about ordering new uniforms and accessories. I knew I'd see my mother there, and I'd be able to explain the situation to her. She would understand; she always understood those things. Then we'd deal with my dad, but the first obstacle was getting out of the house. I fought with my conscience as I decided to wear a shirt over the tank top. I waited until he was occupied with a phone call before saying good bye and hurrying out the door. My plan worked flawlessly, and I made my way to school.

It was like any other morning, except I'd be seeing Troy. My lunch break was during 6th period, and the morning couldn't go quickly enough for me. My third period class was keyboarding, and Mr. Sanders was my teacher, probably my favorite teacher. It's hard to describe him. I can't imagine how many students he had over the years, yet I felt special. The weeks before cheerleading tryouts, I talked to him about them all the time.

I wasn't very proficient with keyboarding, so I used those tryouts as an excuse. I'd tell him I was nervous about making the team, or that my arms were sore. He didn't talk much, but he always had a smile and a kind word. I know it was obvious I was covering up for my lack of skill, but he'd just tell me to do my best and keep trying. Effort was everything in his class; at least that's how I felt.

I remember talking to him that morning. I mentioned the upcoming uniform sale scheduled for that afternoon. I can't remember our exact words; I wish I could.

Spanish followed keyboarding, and I found it harder and harder to focus on schoolwork, counting down to sixth period, and my all important meeting with Troy. It seemed like the biggest thing that would ever happen to me. As the day dragged on, I found myself in my fifth period Science class. Class started around 11:10am. I was nervous, because there was a test scheduled. I intended to study the night before, but the news about Troy took precedence over all other matters. There'd been no time to study, and now I found myself staring blankly at a sheet of questions that may as well have been written in a foreign language. I wished the fire alarm would ring to save me from the situation, and swore that if I found a way out of that jam, I would never allow myself to slack off again.

Chapter 5
A Plunge Into Hell

The science room was on the second floor, right above the cafeteria. About ten minutes into the test, I heard what I thought were rocks being thrown at our windows. My teacher walked over to the window and glanced outside, while the students started to get out of their seats to head towards the window. The teacher said that it was probably a senior prank, and that we were to continue.

As I tried to focus on the questions, I noticed my teacher go into the hallway and talk to another teacher, and I heard what sounded like faint screaming. My teacher came back into the classroom and told everyone to keep down and to get against the wall.

Just then, two teachers, a man and a woman, came into our room with Mr. Sanders. I believe he had one arm over each shoulder and was walking along with them as they shouldered his weight. He was bleeding very badly and fell forward onto the floor, in the middle of the front of the room. There was so much blood, all over. Another teacher came into the room and took off his shirt. He put it on Mr. Sanders to try to stop the bleeding.

My science partner, Bob, knelt down by Mr. Sanders and tried to help him. Around that time, a teacher's aid from another class, Allen, came into the room. I believe he was a junior. Somebody had gotten him to help with Mr. Sanders because Allen knew first aid. Some of the boys took off their shirts, and the shirts were put under Mr. Sanders' head. Allen tried to examine Mr. Sanders' injuries, and Mr. Sanders tried to take off his own shirt, but he couldn't, so Allen cut the shirt off of Mr. Sanders. I could see he'd been shot, and it looked like his shoulder was broken.

My teacher wrote a sign on a white board. It basically said that there was a person dying in our classroom. It was meant to attract attention from the outside world and bring immediate help to Mr. Sanders. He handed the sign to a boy in our class. At first, the boy stood in the window with the sign, but within a few minutes, it was obvious the school was under attack. The boy propped the sign in the window, and got down with the rest of us.

By now, there was really loud screaming coming from somewhere else in the building, the kind that sends a shiver down your spine. It was so loud; it sounded like the screams of a hundred people all at once. It didn't feel real anymore. I don't know how to explain that, but it didn't, yet the realization was pounding in my face, keeping me in the moment and unable to focus on anything else.

I'd just seen Mr. Sanders; he'd been fine; he'd been smiling. Now he was seriously injured with two gunshot wounds. It looked like he had one gunshot to his shoulder and the other through his neck, exiting out his mouth. It looked like part of his jaw was missing, and some of his teeth were broken out. When he tried to talk, I could see his tongue moving. I wasn't thinking anything; I kind of went on autopilot.

The kids moved towards the wall, as the teachers began flipping over the long science tables to make a barricade. I think they must have flipped over eight or so, and some of the kids may have helped. My science room was connected to an adjoining science room.

Somebody opened the door connecting the two rooms, and several of the students from the other room, as well as students from my room, quickly sat in the doorway between our room and theirs, out of view from the hallway door. Some students stayed in the other room. I stayed close to the wall in my science room, frozen in place. Mr. Sanders tried to move towards the wall and ended up in front of the door leading to the hallway, about four or five feet away from me.

That moment was so chaotic, the most unbelievable thing I had ever experienced, until the next. Within seconds, the whole building began to shake, and I heard the unmistakable sound of gunshots and extremely loud screaming. The gunfire was so loud that it didn't seem like normal guns could possibly make that much noise.

The upper half of the door to the science room had a long thin pane of clear glass running vertically along the side near the handle. That window made it possible for the activities within the classroom to be seen from the hallway. The teachers urged us to get beside the wall, behind the tables, so that the room would appear empty to anyone looking in through the door. They told us there were people with guns in the hallway. At that point, I hadn't even comprehended that somebody was prowling the hallways, looking for potential victims, but the realization quickly sank in.

I don't think anybody would have moved or made a sound, anyway. We stayed frozen, silent. Mr. Sanders stayed perfectly still, playing dead. Somebody said they saw a shadow walk by our door and look in the window before moving on. Our room was just two doors down from the library.

At that point, I believe he or they went to the library, because within seconds, we heard gunfire and screaming. It was not like any screaming I had ever heard before or since. It sounded like the kind of screaming you can only picture when people are being tortured. I couldn't stop crying, silently. My body shook violently. I laid frozen to the floor, and the room seemed so cold. I couldn't get a hold of myself; I don't think anybody could.

The gunfire continued, and we heard an extremely loud noise that seemed to be right next to us. There were so many sounds, glass breaking, gunfire, explosions. My mind could only wonder what was actually happening beyond the door. I could feel my body jolt with each shot. My brain stopped working as I lay motionless, unable to think about what was happening around me, unable to move.

All I could think about was yesterday, how I wasted that day. I would never be able to hang out with my mom again. We went out to lunch almost every day of my entire life, but yesterday was the last time, and I couldn't remember telling her that I loved her. I couldn't stop crying, knowing that yesterday was my last chance to tell her how much she meant to me, and I wasted that chance.

I've heard that a person's life flashes before their eyes when they are about to die. I always thought that was a tired cliché, but it really does happen. The parts that mattered flashed in my mind. I saw my family. Mostly, I saw my mother. I realized she was the best friend I ever had; she always was. Growing up, I always had an issue with thinking she would die, and I would have to find a way to live without her. I just kept thinking how odd things were. I had it backwards. She would have to live without me.

Then I thought of my dad. I wished I hadn't worn the tank top. I wasn't a sneaky person, but he'd see the tank top, and he'd see that I lied to him. I wouldn't have the chance to explain things to my mom, so that she could explain it to him. My last act on the planet was defying the two people I loved the most. All I could think was how much I wanted yesterday back, how I would change everything if I could relive that one day.

At some point, the woman teacher grabbed a fire extinguisher and went through the connecting door to put out a fire. I'm not sure how she knew about the fire, but when she came back, I think she said that the chemical lab had been bombed. I don't think I can ever explain how scared I was, terrified, petrified.

After what seemed like 20 minutes or so, the sounds of gunfire stopped. There was silence, a sick silence. We all stayed frozen, quiet and still, for about five minutes. Then the unmistakable sounds began again, and I braced myself for another round, but they lasted just a minute or two, at the most. Then nothing.

Chapter 6
The Day That Wouldn't End

At that time, Mr. Sanders was still cognitive. One of the students stood up to look out the window, and Mr. Sanders yelled for him to get down. He was still looking after us. I remember thinking that he was still our teacher, and we were safe, because he was taking care of us. I don't like to think about that. It makes me cry, even now.

About 20 minutes after the gunfire stopped, the fire alarms started to blare. They were so loud, that they did the unimaginable. They made the most unbelievably horrible experience a person could ever imagine, worse. We stayed frozen, listening to those blaring alarms, for what must have been an hour, listening, still. At some point, we began to hear helicopters overhead, so we knew the community was aware of what was happening.

I'm not sure of the exact sequence of the next series of events. It's hard to get them straight in my mind, but Allen, the teacher's aid, called his father from the classroom telephone, and Allen's dad called 911 on a three way call, hoping to get help. That three way call became our link to the outside world.

The operator said to put a red shirt on the outside doorknob, in the hallway, so that the SWAT team could find us easier. We were terrified to do that, because, at that point, we thought the gunmen still had control of the school. Otherwise, the police would have gotten to us by then. We'd done our best to stay out of view of the hallway and to stay out of sight. The red shirt would alert anybody in the hallway that there were potential victims within the science room, but we did it. I don't know exactly who had the courage to open that door and tie the red shirt on the handle, but someone did. We were desperate for help.

It was important to keep Mr. Sanders as warm as possible, so he wouldn't go into shock. He was so white at that point; he'd lost so much blood. Somebody grabbed the blanket from the fire box on the wall, and all the boys who were wearing undershirts took off their shirts to cover him. I believe some of the boys had already taken off their shirts to help Mr. Sanders, but now all the others joined in.

Somewhere during that timeframe, we realized there was a television in the classroom, a fairly large set that was suspended from the ceiling and visible to most of us. Somebody turned it on, without the sound, but the subtitles were scrolling across the screen, so we could read what they were saying. I was about 10-12 feet away and could see it perfectly.

The local stations were showing live scenes from outside our school. At first, everyone was intently watching, but there wasn't any real information. It was just general scenes from the helicopters and interviews with people that didn't know anything. I believe most of the people in our room stopped watching the television. It seemed like a few people were whispering amongst themselves, or maybe even talking to themselves. Some people seemed out of it.

My eyes stayed fixed on the TV; I'm not sure why. After about 10 minutes, the television camera focused on the cafeteria door. I'll never forget that moment, and I have never seen the clip since. It was live footage. The camera zoomed in on the cafeteria door; obviously the cameraman saw something I didn't, and I squinted and leaned in closer to see. At first, I couldn't see anything newsworthy. Then I realized that there was an enormous amount of blood seeping out from underneath that door. It looked like a gallon of spilt milk had oozed under the door to the outside, forming a huge puddle of the deepest red blood, so much blood. It was horrifying. I heard myself gasp along with at least five or six other people. Then everybody in the room snapped to attention and leaned in to focus on the picture, but the scene changed quickly.

Soon we saw a boy coming out of the window to the library while rescuers waited below. I didn't recognize him, but other people did.

People were saying, "Oh my God! Oh my God!"

Almost everybody began to cry uncontrollably. It was clear that the siege was huge, and it was horrendous. My eyes were watering so badly that I couldn't read the text on the screen anymore. At some point, the television showed 3 boys had been stopped running through a field, and I wondered if they were involved in the shootings. I didn't know what the scene meant, but I was praying it was a sign the attack had ended. There was a scene of someone on the roof, and it turned out to be the janitor. At the time, I thought it might be a gunman.

By then, it seemed like hours had gone by. The SWAT team hadn't come. Still, the fire alarms blared. The noise was making everyone crazy, and Mr. Sanders began to lose consciousness. Bob and Allen took out Mr. Sanders' wallet and showed him pictures of his family. You just can't tell how a person will react under stress. Bob and Allen sat by his side the entire time, showing him pictures, talking about his family, keeping him conscious.

They would take out a picture and ask, "Who is this?"

Mr. Sanders would answer. Then Bob or Allen would ask questions about the person, and Mr. Sanders would say something nice about each one. The boys did their best to keep the conversation going. It went on and on.

At some point, the alarms stopped, but I could still hear ringing in my ears. It had been almost four hours since Mr. Sanders entered our room. It seemed like hours since 911 had been made aware of our location. For those hours, I was sure that the SWAT team would be rescuing us at any minute. I sat waiting, anticipating. Suddenly, we heard screaming coming from the adjacent science room. Men dressed in black and carrying guns rushed into our room and began screaming at us.

I thought that now I was going to die; I thought they were the gunmen. We all must have thought that, because everyone in the room began to scream. They said they were SWAT and showed us the writing on the back of their shirts. I hadn't seen that until they pointed it out, and at that point, it didn't do much to calm me down. They instructed us to put our hands behind our heads and follow them in a single file. They kept their guns pointed directly at us the entire time.

We didn't want to leave without Mr. Sanders, but they insisted that they needed a bed to evacuate him. The SWAT team moved quickly, and we went down the hallway to the stairs. There are two sections to that stairway. We hurried down the stairway to the landing in the middle, facing the library, and we gathered there.

Along the way, I caught a glimpse of the aftermath. Lockers were riddled with bullets. The window to the library was shattered, and glass littered the ground. It was such a sharp contrast to the perfect hallway I traveled on my way into the classroom. It was like somebody changed the scenery while I waited on the other side of the door. I remember thinking that.

The SWAT team continued to point their guns at us. One thing I'll always remember is running past a bucket with a sponge and soapy water. It was next to a blood stain. That has always bothered me. It always stuck in my head that somebody thought it was more important to clean up the blood, than to get us out and save Mr. Sanders. I hate that picture, but it's stuck in my head.

We waited on the landing in the middle of the staircase until the last of us had arrived, Allen. He'd been the last one to leave the room, not wanting to leave without Mr. Sanders. As soon as Allen arrived, the SWAT team instructed us to move quickly down the stairs and through the cafeteria.

We ran out through the cafeteria. It was like a ghost town. You could see empty tables with half eaten lunches everywhere. Backpacks were still sitting where their owners had left them. The floor was under about four inches of water, flooded from the sprinklers. In some areas of the building, the sprinklers must have turned on, but I had no idea of that, until we had descended the staircase. The science room sprinklers hadn't turned on, and I remember thinking how lucky we were that we didn't have to lay in the cold water all that time.

I was wearing open toed sandals with heels, and the water was freezing and slick. Even though they were there to help, I was terrified of the SWAT team as they barked instructions and aimed their weapons at us. We made our way through the cafeteria to the door leading to the outside.

There, a member of the SWAT team held the door and stopped each of us as we arrived. He said to wait two seconds after the person ahead of us left the doorway. They wanted to space us out, in case someone was still targeting the school. That way, nobody could take out a group of students before the police could react. After arriving at the door, I waited until the SWAT officer tapped my back and instructed me to go. The entire time, we held our hands clasped behind our heads.

After exiting the building from the doorway, I hurried straight ahead, and then up the concrete steps. My slick sandals were sopping wet. I remember hearing the slosh of the leather, and feeling one foot slip underneath me, but I kept moving.

I ran past two dead bodies. Bodies don't look quite like they do in movies. It is unspeakable. There was blood everywhere, a weird look on their faces, and a weird color to their skin. They lay in unnatural positions that leave an imprint on your brain.

The girl in front of me froze upon seeing the bodies. She stopped in her tracks, and the SWAT officer began screaming for her to move. Their guns were fixed on us, and I remember pushing her in the back to get her to move. I was still so scared.

Chapter 7
The Aftermath

We ran to a back corner of the school, near the dumpsters. A police car was waiting. They drove us, four at a time, to a safe area in Clement Park. I was in the first carload of people from my classroom to be taken to the park.

Once there, we were examined by paramedics. I'd worn pantyhose to school that day, to make me look thinner. The waistband of the pantyhose rose well above the waistband of my black pants, and I was embarrassed. The paramedic was incredibly handsome, and I couldn't get past that. Then, I felt ashamed. Here I was thinking about how I looked to this paramedic, and people died. How was that possible? Who cares about the way they look at a time like that? The day just would not stop.

We sat at the park for the longest time, and it started to sink in, and I felt bad. I don't know why, but I did. I kept telling myself that I was okay, that nothing really even happened to me. I should feel sorry for the people who were hurt, because I was okay. I was lucky; I should be helping other people instead of getting help, but for some reason, I could barely move.

After awhile, a bus took us to Leawood Elementary School, just a few blocks from Columbine, so that our parents could pick us up. On the bus, I borrowed a friend's shirt, because I didn't want my parents to see my tank top. I felt like a bad person. Here these other people are hurt, and I'm worried about what my parents might think of my outfit? I expected better of myself.

Upon arriving at the elementary school, we were lined up on the stage, six at a time. They announced our names so our parents could see us. Then we were questioned by the FBI. At some point during that time, somebody told me that the police had actually been the ones who set off the alarms in the building. It was a tactic intended to disorient the gunmen.

The policeman offered to call my family. It was probably 4:15 or 4:30 by then, and it was the first chance I had to talk to anybody. I called my dad's cell phone. He'd been working within a construction project of newly built homes the entire day, and wasn't even aware of the ordeal that I'd been through. The line kept breaking up, and he didn't understand what had happened. It probably should have bothered me, but at that point, I figured somebody would show up eventually. I should have called my mom instead, because she was already looking for me, but had no idea where I was or how to find me.

My mother and Aunt Theresa had been taking care of my grandmother that entire day. She lived in a nursing home on the north side of town. Every Tuesday they took her out and did special things for her. She didn't have a television and never listened to the radio. They hadn't seen the news or even heard about the shootings until about 2pm. They both got home around the same time, and they had answering machines full of messages from relatives.

At that point, my mom had no idea how to find me. All the area schools were on lockdown. That meant that the students could not be released until a parent or guardian arrived to get them. After making numerous phone calls, my mother went to Ken Caryl Middle School to get Sarah and David. All the while, she kept an eye out for me, hoping that I had somehow left the school earlier in the day.

Some of the kids from Columbine had gotten out of the building long before me, and they had begun to show up in several different places. There were small groups of kids gathering at the mall and fast food restaurants in my area. Some of the Columbine students began to show up at area schools, to pick up younger brothers and sisters affected by the lock down. My mother ran into a friend of mine while picking up Sarah and David at Ken Caryl Middle School.

She told my mother she had seen me at least an hour before, and that I was safe, but she had no idea where to find me at that point. My mother's worst fears were calmed, but she was still concerned that I had not called her or called home. She was afraid I was in shock or the like, wandering the streets, but she never dreamed I was still inside that school building.

As soon as Aunt Theresa had picked up her sons at their elementary school, she joined my mother in the search. Aunt Joanne came to help soon afterwards. They had no idea where to start. My mother frantically called every person she could think of who might possibly have information about me. Surprisingly, several different people said they had seen me, but nobody could remember where. As the day dragged on, she began to panic.

The roads were crowded in the middle of the day. Everybody was looking for their loved ones. My mom and her sisters kept hearing conflicting information. They had been to several different places by the time Aunt Joanne heard that the police were transporting the evacuated students to Leawood Elementary.

They had no reason to believe I was there. Other people reported seeing me early in the afternoon, but by then it was after 5pm, and my family was becoming increasingly worried. Aunt Joanne set out to Leawood Elementary.

Leawood had a frenzied atmosphere. Many of the parents had gone to other locations first, and they were frantic by the time they got there. Everyone was worried about their kids and asking us if we'd seen this person or that. I couldn't remember who I had seen and who I hadn't, or where I had seen them.

In the hallway, I saw Troy. He ran up to me and gave me a hug. We didn't speak; we just stood there holding each other. I'd never even spoken to him before. My day was better. We went outside until Aunt Joanne came to get me.

I remember her saying, "We've been looking everywhere for you." I began to cry and collapsed in her arms.

After I got home, I started watching the news. There is a clip they kept showing on TV, a long line of students running from the building with their hands clasped behind their heads. I cringed every time I saw it, because just about every time they showed it, they showed the part with me running. Remember my outfit, I'm in a blue tank top and black pants; I'm behind the girl in the leather jacket. I wore a shirt over that top as I left the house, and I had another shirt covering that top when Aunt Joanne picked me up, but the camera recorded the outfit I actually wore to school. It still bothers me that I wore it, and it bothers me that something so silly bothers me.

I watched the news coverage of parents picking up their kids. I recall thinking how sad it must have been to be one of the parents who couldn't find their child. There they were, gathering together, waiting for word, hoping that somehow their child had ended up at a different school or had gotten out of the building long before the police began transporting the survivors to Leawood Elementary.

As the hours went by, I figured the parents still looking must have had the children who were shot or killed. I was just so sad for them. I hated that was how people would find out their child had passed away. I would never want my parents to find out that way. After awhile, I stopped watching. It hurt too much; the happy reunions had ceased, and there was nothing left but desperation.

I hadn't eaten all day, and my family kept encouraging me to eat, but I couldn't. I couldn't picture ever eating again. I had the worst stomach ache I'd ever felt and was nauseated at the same time. My head was pounding, and I couldn't focus. It seemed like forever since I'd slept, like I'd been gone for days, so I went to bed.

I laid there thinking I would never be able to sleep, that I would probably never sleep again, but within minutes, I was out. I slept until the next morning, never even stirred. I was drained, totally drained. I kept telling myself that nothing happened to me. I was lucky. Other people were the victims, not me. The aftermath was almost as surreal as the actual tragedy. I didn't even know Mr. Sanders had passed away until the next day. I was so sure they could save him. How could they not save him? How could God let him die when Allen and Bob worked so hard to keep him safe?

At that time, we weren't sure how many people had actually died in the tragedy. There weren't any set numbers regarding the injuries and how badly people were hurt. The papers and newscasts were full of estimates and gory details. It was so confusing and unreal. I don't think I wanted to accept the truth, because it made no sense. I kept thinking that the estimates must be an exaggeration. I stopped reading the newspapers and tried to avoid the coverage on the television.

Reporters began calling. They wouldn't leave me alone. I gave just one interview, and it ended up on the second page. I had no great words of wisdom. I just survived. People were hurt; people were killed. I felt very small and insignificant in the world. I sat in that classroom while all hell broke loose, and it seemed like it made no difference. I hadn't saved anybody, not even myself. It was sheer luck, and knowing that terrified me. I couldn't imagine why anyone would want to hear what I had to say.

It's hard to describe the feelings I had in the aftermath. History assigns a name to huge events to try to sum up everything that happened in the tiniest of terms, a neat little package. The names assigned to shooting sprees usually include the words massacre or siege. We hear of battles and wars, but not here. It was a tragedy, a true tragedy. That one word describes the entire event to a tee.

Everybody hurt; everybody lost, and the community set out trying to make pink lemonade from the bitterest of lemons. That was probably the first sign that things had changed; I had changed. I didn't want to find a moral in this. I didn't want to learn a lesson or someday say that good came from this. I thought we were screwed. I was not going to be the pink lemonade girl, to cheer for Columbine. No good could ever come from a tragedy. I cried for Columbine.

I felt sorry for the people who lost their lives, and for the injured people, and for everyone who knew and loved them. I couldn't fathom that one day they would say that the lessons learned were worth the pain endured. Maybe some can, but they're better people than me.

I felt sorry for the students and for the teachers. I felt sorry for Mr. Sanders and his family. I felt sorry for myself, and my friends, and our parents, and I felt sorry for the parents of the gunmen, and for the people who loved them. It must be the most horrendous feeling, and nobody wants to hear about their pain, but no one would ever want to endure it.

Chapter 8
Defending Columbine and Other Strange Twists

The world doesn't stop; the clocks don't miss a beat. I never knew that. I don't know what I thought before that day, but now I know that no matter how horrible the situation, the clock keeps ticking and somehow, somewhere, life goes on. That broke my heart, but the world reached out, and the community embraced us.

There was so much sorrow. There were memorial services and funerals. I went to two of the funerals. I didn't know them well, but my friends did, and I wanted to be there, because I cared. I cared about my friends, and I cared about their friends. That was so present in the front of my mind, how much a person can care about people they hardly ever knew, or even didn't know at all. It all seemed so personal, like I'd lost my own family members, distant cousins I hardly knew. It was like someone had walked into our house and gunned them down during a family reunion. Now I'd never get to know them. I felt a loss not knowing them, like the world lost something huge by not getting to know these important, unique people better, but it was too late.

My friends and I didn't talk about that day. We hugged, and held hands, and talked about the weather, and didn't talk at all. I really don't know how anyone else felt. Maybe we were all too fragile to face reality, or maybe we were too afraid to invade each other's space, but it hung in the air. We just never acknowledged its presence.

People made quilts, so many quilts that every student got at least one. My family gathered near, and my mother's family closed ranks around me. There were teddy bears and beanie babies, cards and phone calls. Everyone went out of their way to make us feel safe and loved, and it helped.

By then, the police had named the gunmen, Dylan Klebold and Eric Harris, two seniors who had attended Columbine High School. They believed those two young men actually tried to blow up the school. Immediately, my mind focused on what little I knew of them first hand.

There was a group of kids at school that stood out from the rest. They hung out in the back of the cafeteria wearing heavy trench coats and army boots. They wore odd black hats, berets, like a military hat or an artist's cap. They wore black coke bottle glasses and camouflage pants. They called themselves The Trenchcoat Mafia. I really didn't know them. I can't ever remember even seeing Eric Harris at school, but I knew who Dylan was.

He was an awkward boy, over six feet tall, and was very thin with reddish blond hair. He kind of walked towards the wall, away from the crowd. Dylan was thin, almost frail; I'd seen one guy walk by him and intentionally bump his shoulder with theirs, hard, painful. Once, I'd seen somebody throw a coke can at him, and I heard people laugh at him a couple of times.

I didn't stick up for him. As far as I know, nobody did. I felt sorry for him, but I'd been teased before, and other kids got teased. I hadn't seen it happen more than a couple of times, so I never gave it much thought, until the media picked up on it.

Then came the insinuations, the accusations. There were rumors that the jocks at Columbine had bullied and terrorized the gunmen and their friends. Here we were trying to keep walking, to cope with the unthinkable, and it felt like some people were trying to find a reason why it was our own fault. Maybe that wasn't the intent, but it felt that way.

I found myself trying to think up reasons why the violence against our school was unacceptable. There was bullying, nobody would deny that, but not all of the athletes were bullies. Most of the victims weren't even athletes. The gunmen were seniors. Everybody in the school that day was a target; they weren't selective. How could the incoming freshmen have terrorized them for years? It made no sense.

At the time, it felt like the harshest of criticism by people who didn't have a clue. I was a sophomore who barely knew anybody at the school, but I was now a cheerleader. I knew some of the jocks, and they were regular kids. There were definitely people who picked on other people, but they weren't the majority. They weren't Columbine.

I know long before I was ever born, movies have depicted some jocks picking on less popular kids in high school and even college, so it didn't start with Columbine, and it certainly didn't define the vast majority of students there. It felt like we were being labeled a school of bullies and malcontents. We became the subject of internet chat rooms and worldwide debate. Everybody had an opinion, yet didn't know us first hand, and that hurt.

Within a week, details of the shooting were becoming very concrete. Thirteen people had been killed by the gunmen. The two gunmen apparently killed themselves, and 23 people had been wounded badly enough to require hospitalization.

The police found bombs in the school building that had not detonated. Apparently, Klebold and Harris intended to blow up the cafeteria, and the rest of the school right along with it. There were propane tanks that never exploded.

Fifth period was lunch time for about one third of the students at Columbine. There were three different lunch periods, so there was a good chance a large percentage of the school would have been in that immediate area. The cafeteria sits directly below the science room, where I had been during the rampage. My mind kept racing throughout those days. There was just too much information coming from all sides.

The more information that was released, the more questions there were. Somehow, these two young men managed to get those bombs into the school. Maybe the school should have had more security, but it is a school. Columbine has an open campus. It seemed like everybody wanted to debate the issues, and in debating the issues, I couldn't help but feel like the focus was taken away from the victims. I know it's easy for me to say, and that the community and the people in authority needed to look at those issues, but at the time, it just seemed so cold. I felt like the entire focus should have been on the victims, and there is just no good answer to that.

Then my happy little family started to crumble. Now, I've thought about this a lot, because it's so important to me. I guess there were cracks in the foundation of my home life before the tragedy ever occurred. After the move to Colorado, my parents didn't seem to get along as well as when we lived in Idaho, but we still functioned. We were managing, but after that day at Columbine, everything changed.

My father is a veteran, the recipient of medals and awards. He was wounded in action in Vietnam, sustaining several wounds from gunshot and shrapnel. I'd seen his wounds; they were hard to miss, but I didn't know about his pain. He carried those scars on the inside. He never talked about it. I guess he couldn't, until that day. Looking back, the change was almost instantaneous, but all eyes were on me.

He wasn't home much, and when he was, I could almost feel his anger. He spoke of the war, and it was ugly. It seemed that he held it close at hand, like a snapshot that had always been buried in a drawer and suddenly reappeared. Now he kept it in his pocket, and he looked at it all the time, but I didn't see that back then.

I had a new group of friends. We shared a common bond. I began to see Troy on a regular basis, and I met his group of friends. It was a blessing, like leaving behind my past, but staying close to people I'd seen there. I think it got me through those days.

A local movie theater opened their doors to us, allowing us an evening to watch movies for free. People went out of their way to be kind, and everyday schedules became a thing of the past for awhile. I stayed up late and slept in till noon. By the time school restarted, I was ready to focus on something else.

On May 3, 1999, not two weeks after the shootings, we returned to school, not Columbine High School, but Chatfield Senior High. Chatfield was Columbine's arch rival. For years, the schools battled for superiority on the academic and athletic fronts. It was not a friendly rivalry as much as a grudge match, until the shootings. Chatfield opened their arms to Columbine. They welcomed us.

Columbine's school colors are dark blue and silver; Chatfield's are dark red and silver. Chatfield's hallways were covered in blue and silver. There were signs and banners, and some kids were even wearing t-shirts combining the two schools' colors. Some of the kids from Chatfield stayed past their scheduled dismissal time to make sure the incoming students from Columbine didn't get lost. We were family, rivals, fierce competitors on the football fields, but brothers standing side by side when times were tough. It meant so much. It meant the world.

My cousin, Michael, was a student at Chatfield. At that time, we didn't know each other very well, hardly at all, but he insisted that I share his locker at school. In that locker, he had tucked away flowers and other welcoming gifts for my first day back to school. He showed me around, and he did everything possible to be a shoulder to lean on when I needed it most. I'm not sure I ever really thanked him. I think I walked around in a daze, going through the motions of life without really letting it sink in. It was like I was surrounded by this invisible barrier, a force field. I could see the world moving around me, and I could pretend to move along with it, but I was in my own little space, and that was okay with them, and it helped.

Chatfield students went to classes in the morning, and Columbine students went in the afternoon. Columbine teachers set up classes in the borrowed building, and life went on. It was a good thing. We needed that.

Chapter 9
The New World – For Better or Worse

My new school schedule was a strain on my family, though. My younger sister and brother remained on their early to school, early dismissal schedule, while I didn't start classes till well after noon, and wasn't dismissed until 6pm. We had always eaten dinner as a family; and it ended with the start of that schedule. It changed our family life, but I never noticed, another crack in the foundation.

Throughout that time, there were rumors and reports of a third gunman still roaming our streets, targeting the athletes and cheerleaders. I thought that people I never knew were somehow targeting me for something I hadn't done. I was scared to go out, unwilling to stay home.

It seemed like everyday there were at least one or two stories focusing on the investigation, or the lawsuits, or controversies involving memorials erected in the park. We were surrounded in sorrow, and it was news. Then there was a school shooting in Georgia, only about a month after our ordeal.

I was in line at the local grocery store, buying ingredients to make a cake, when I heard someone say it was a copycat of Columbine. It felt like a bucket of cold water had been thrown in my dazed and confused face; like I'd been zoning out, focusing on the trivial, then snapped instantly back into reality.

It was so awful. The world was becoming a terrifying place to live, and there was no where else to go. I wanted to cry, to scream out loud enough for everyone on the planet to stop this insanity, but I knew it wouldn't matter. Hundreds of thousands of people were already crying, screaming out that same message, and another high school sat in devastation.

I remember standing in that line, staring at the metal handles of the little red basket I was holding. I kept looking at the cake mix and eggs, and I literally didn't know what to do. I didn't know whether to stay in line or just set the basket down and leave, like suddenly I had some huge decision to make. Looking back, I can't imagine what the people around me must have thought. I just walked towards the door, and left the basket and its contents on the customer service counter. I didn't say anything to anyone. I didn't know what else to do.

There were mental health services available, and I went to see a counselor several times, but she asked way too many questions. She wanted all the gory details, and I felt invaded. I owned those memories and was not ready to share them with anyone. I wasn't even sure if I could ever look at them again. I wanted to hide them in the same drawer where my father kept his memories of Vietnam, tucked away until I could bear to look at them, but the counselor pushed on, and I stopped going, and I stopped talking.

By the end of May, the school year had ended. Any sense of a schedule ended right along with it. There was nowhere I had to be, so there was nothing to keep me on track. I think people walked on eggshells around me, afraid to upset an already troubled girl.

My mother had always been my best friend and confidante, but I stopped talking to her. I didn't want to talk to anyone. I wanted to deny any effect that day may have had on me. Life at home was full of heartache and trauma. My parents were no longer the perfect couple that I remembered.

The atmosphere was tense, but it was hard to put my finger on the actual problem. I didn't even try. I just shut it out. I feel bad about that now. I always promised my little brother that I'd be there for him, but I wasn't. I stayed out as much as possible and knew that I could. Everyone wanted me to heal, whatever it took.

It was hard to keep going. It seemed like everywhere I went, there were reminders. Columbine High School is on Pierce Street. It is a main thoroughfare in my little area of Littleton. I had to keep driving by Columbine to get anywhere.

Often I'd drive by the school, only to see people standing in front of the Columbine High School sign while somebody took their picture, like it was a tourist attraction. I don't know why that bothered me so much. It wasn't like they were saying it was okay or anything like that, but it just bugged me.

There was one scene that kept replaying in my mind, every time I drove by that school, until I finally refused to drive down Pierce at all. There was a window on the first floor of Columbine that was stained in blood, not a splatter or splotch, but hand prints. Two hands were imprinted on the glass, and there were streaks of blood where those hands had slid down the window. It was so awful. I could almost see it happening, even though I hadn't seen anything like that actually happen. Day after day, I'd see those imprints and wonder whose they were. I'd wonder how long it would take for someone, anyone to go into the building and clean them. I'd think of the parents; sometimes it made me cry. I felt like it was so disrespectful, so wrong. Finally, I refused to watch. I refused to drive down that street until they cleaned that window.

Clement Park is right next to the school on an adjacent main street. To avoid driving down Pierce, I often found myself on Bowles, the street that runs directly in front of Clement Park. I'd constantly be driving by the flowers and signs. As much as it helped, knowing that everyone cared, it reminded me of that day. It seemed like my mind raced constantly, from one thing to the next, almost like I was looking for something on which to fixate, completely oversensitive.

I felt like the community wanted to show support and be strong by wearing t-shirts and sporting bumper stickers, but I also felt bitter that it was beginning to become a fashion statement. People talked about it in the grocery stores and fast food restaurants, everybody but the people who had been in the school when it happened. There was just no escaping that day or its memories.

I couldn't sleep anymore. I felt like I couldn't talk, and it made me angry. Sarah was afraid to start school at Columbine in the fall. She thought it was haunted and that the gunmen's ghosts roamed the library. It was a rumor she heard, and she couldn't shake it from her mind. That made me angry. I thought she was just looking for attention. Now I feel bad about that. I never talked to Sarah about my experience. I'm not sure if anybody ever talked to the incoming freshmen about it. It felt like they were intruding on a club that didn't want new members. It must have been hard for them, but at the time, I'm not sure any of us were thinking about that.

My mom was always stressed; you could see it. I didn't want to add any more to her plate by telling her details of what happened to me. All she knew was where I was during the shootings, and that Mr. Sanders died. That's all she ever knew, until now.

I didn't want to burden my father with my memories. He had his own. He'd seen gunfire and explosions first hand. He hadn't tried to reach out to me about my ordeal, and I assumed he would've tried to help me if he could. I figured the suffering I'd been though was bringing back memories for him, and he didn't seem to be handling those memories well, so I never spoke to him about it.

Chapter 10
Reality Sets In

It must have been so hard for him, our protector. He couldn't camp out in front of the door anymore, like he'd done for Sarah when we were little. The monsters were real, and they looked just like everyone else. I have to think other parents felt that way, but I don't know. I just know that the father I remember would have done anything to keep his daughters safe and that he thought the biggest threat to us were the boys who called the house. After the tragedy, he never had the luxury of thinking the media was painting a picture more gruesome than reality could ever be. He'd seen violence first hand; the media could never outdo the truth.

I knew that I had to keep this to myself and try to get over it. I had a stomach ache for months, and it never really went away. It felt like my stomach muscles never stopped clenching. I took long hot baths trying to loosen them up, but within minutes, it was back. I had horrible nightmares. I still do. They were so real. I'd never seen anything so real before, violence so vivid that I'd jolt up during a deep sleep, finding myself in a sitting position when I awoke. I used to wake up crying every night, in a cold sweat. At that time, my mom slept in my room, on a futon, because she was afraid to sleep in the same room with my dad. I believe he was having night terrors too, but trying to shake them off.

I remember thinking that I had to be extremely quiet, so that she wouldn't know I was upset. The only thing harder for me than being sad, is thinking my mom is sad. I kept it all a secret, how scared I was, how depressed I was. I used to think that I had become a very strong person by holding it all in, but then I'd think maybe I had just become very mean and cold. My temper was so bad it scared me, and I had no patience with the world.

When the year books came out, the press was trying to buy them. They were offering as much as $5,000. I wouldn't sell mine; I thought it was selling out. Now, I'm not sure what happened to it. Maybe it's lost, or I just forget where I put it, but I can't find it, and it's probably for the best. I'm not ready to look at it anyway.

During the summer, I had cheerleading practice a lot. It seemed as though we kept focusing our attention on the tragedy. We did several fund raisers, and we were supposed to be giving back to the community. I felt that I wasn't over what happened to me enough to give back. I hated it. Everything we did seemed to be about that day. Even our uniforms had the columbine flower on them. It was a constant reminder, and I felt so much anger, because I was expected to wrap myself in the most horrific experience of my life. I don't know if anyone else felt that way. I never mentioned it, before now.

We attended cheer camp with the Jr. Varsity Squad. They were the incoming freshmen and could not have been in the school on April 20th. We had a game where balloons had to pop. Some of them started to cry because they thought it was gunfire. Several of the junior team members cried at certain songs on the radio, because it made them think of that day. It made me angry. They had no clue. They didn't hear the gunfire or have any idea what it was like to be there that day. I felt like everyone was trying to get attention for our pain, and I thought I was the only one who felt that way. I didn't want to cheer anymore, but I was on the team, and I wasn't a quitter.

The new school year started on August 16, 1999 with a big assembly. It was intended to help the students and teachers get off to a fresh start and bring us together as a school. I don't remember much about it. It was like we were going through the motions, trying to prove to ourselves and each other that the events which happened just a few months before couldn't change who we were, and they wouldn't ruin the school for its rightful occupants. It was like reclaiming that land. I didn't want to go, but I had to if I was ever going to be able to go again.

The next day I read a story in the local newspaper. Towards the end of the article, there was a snippet about me, specifically citing that I had not gotten to bed until the early hours of the morning. It basically said that I was not afraid, but I was up late because I applied a self tanner, and it hadn't dried.

I was blown away. Maybe it looked like nothing bothered me, and I was just some silly teenage girl focusing only on her tan, but I was scared to go back. It was hard to go back. I thought I was one of the bravest people I'd ever met going back to that place.

I've often wondered if I really seemed that nonchalant, or if that reporter just wanted to end the story on a high note. Either way, it bummed me out, and I felt bad about myself. I could imagine the injured students and their parents reading that story and thinking that life was back to normal for everyone but them, that nobody even thought about them anymore. I couldn't even imagine what the parents of the murdered children might think. They would think that life was so normal, that I had no worries on that first day of school except for the way that I looked. It seemed so disrespectful to the victims, and I was the poster child.

The last thing I ever wanted to do was bring grief to people who had more than enough already. I hoped they hadn't read the part of the article about me. I searched my brain over and over to try to remember exactly what I had said, but I honestly couldn't recall. I think it's wrong to interview a person at a time like that, when their mind is on autopilot.

I was glad I hadn't been interviewed right after the tragedy, while I was being examined by the paramedic. That reporter might have written that the four hours I spent lying on the freezing cold floor, watching my life flash before my eyes, and my favorite teacher slip away, was nothing compared to the embarrassment I felt having my pantyhose sticking up above my waistband. It made me wonder how accurate the rest of the news stories were. Were they reporting Columbine or painting a picture that would make people want to read the paper? The coverage continued. Day after day, the paper seemed to be filled with stories, and I looked at them a little differently, just the right balance of tragedy and hope. Was that coincidence or engineered? I never wanted to talk to a reporter again.

It was hard going back to that school. There were conspicuously new lockers replacing the old ones that had been riddled with bullets. There was a wall blocking the view of the old library, but I knew it was still there, hollow and empty. There was new drywall on the walls that had been marred with blood and gunshots. It was all so creepy. People seemed meaner; the clicks became tighter, and everyone stayed with their own groups. School was colder; nobody talked about things at all.

Cheerleading practice was my last class period every day, and I just didn't want to go anymore. I didn't want to be a part of it. It all seemed pointless, and the fun was gone. The team was focused on competitions, and the practices became grueling. It was hard to keep up the pace.

The gym was closed, damaged from the water that flooded the school during the attack. Sarah was on the gymnastic team, and they had to practice in the evenings at a school gym quite a ways from our house. Dinners together were a thing of the past. Family Sundays were ancient history, and all resemblances to the family we had been were gone, but we kept acting like that was temporary, like somehow things would get back to normal at any moment, but they never did.

By then, Troy and I were no longer dating, but I still had my new group of friends, and they were my lifeline. I met a boy who changed my life. Brad is an incredible person; we actually dated for awhile. After a few months, we stopped dating and became great friends. He was my link to the goodness of Columbine. We'd both experienced the tragedy, in different ways, and he never judged. We never asked for details of that day, and we never gave any to each other. It is a huge comfort to have a friend like that, and it helped a great deal.

Chapter 11
A Missed Step

During that time, my family began to unravel. My father had a series of heart attacks and had surgery performed at the Veteran's Hospital, about an hour or so from our house. There was no quick route to that hospital, but all of us went to visit every day that he was there. I was scared; I didn't want him to die. I didn't used to think about that kind of thing, but at that point, it was all I could think about.

My world came crashing down in mid January of that year. One morning, after we went to school, my mother fled the house in only her stocking feet. She ran to a payphone outside of a local grocery store. She called my aunt for help, and later that day, she went about collecting her children. I never saw that coming. I was called to the office that afternoon and given the message to meet my mother at my aunt's house. Once there, the world as I knew it ceased to exist.

My mother was afraid of my father, afraid of what he might do to her. She said there was a violent episode between the two of them after we children had left for school, and she felt that she could never go back. That was our new reality. We stowed away at a cheap hotel for several days, missing school, and the world went on, and I missed a step, and I started to fall behind.

After about a week or so, we returned to school, and my mother set about trying to work out some arrangement with my dad. She didn't have a dime, and she was afraid to touch the money in their bank accounts, so she borrowed from family, and moved into Aunt Joanne's basement.

Aunt Joanne's family went out of their way to be nice, but it was so hard. We needed our stuff, and our space, and I wanted to believe that my parents would reunite. My mother never made us feel badly if we chose to stay with our father. She just felt she wasn't safe.

I stayed with my dad, trying to get our little family back together. I visited my mom everyday, but I felt myself slipping behind, losing touch. I wanted to act like things hadn't changed. I still lived in the family home, but my family was gone. My father and I would rent movies, and watch TV, and go through the motions. I would have given anything to have back what I took for granted just a year before, to turn back the clock, and somehow I tricked myself into believing it was possible. I thought that I could be the liaison between my two favorite people, but it was a pipe dream. My mother said she was afraid of him. Nothing I ever said could change that.

Before the break-up, I wanted a car more than anything else in the world, but there was no money for a big purchase like that. In fact, in the months before they separated, my mother had a hard time scrounging together enough money for school clothes, but within days of my return to the family home, my dad bought a late model, used jeep.

I never wanted a jeep. In fact, that was the last vehicle on the planet I would have chosen. I never really considered it to be mine, but my brother and sister thought it was mine. It was the beginning of what would prove to be the longest war in the history of our family. The process of divide and conquer had begun. I just couldn't see that, and I'm not sure it would have made any difference if I had.

Looking back, it must have been unbelievably hard for my mother to watch. I drove that jeep in front of her as she borrowed pennies from her sisters, but she never judged, and she refused to cry, at least in front of us. She just kept walking, trying to make lemonade as her marriage crumbled, and her world fell apart.

After a few weeks, my mother got her own apartment. It was a very small 2 bedroom place on the second story of an old apartment building, but it was close to the schools. It was the oldest building in the area. They had no air conditioning, cable, or internet, and as my mother, and brother, and sister set up their household, I knew things would never be the same. I thought the world would stop right then and there, but it just kept moving.

It seemed like everybody else's lives moved smoothly, and ours had begun to spiral out of control, like a huge black cloud settled over us the morning I chose that blue tank top and headed down the road to Columbine High School. Now there was nothing left but impossible choices and learning to cope. I stayed with my father, living a comfortable life, and worrying about my family. I was afraid he might die, and I didn't want him to die alone.

In February of 2000, right around Valentines Day, a friend of mine and his girlfriend were shot to death while he worked at a local sandwich shop. The restaurant was just a few blocks down the street from Columbine. His name was Nick, and he was my food partner at school. We were in a class where we learned how to cook, and he was in my group. Nick was a year younger than me, kind of shy, and very cute, just a very nice and friendly boy. Then he was gone. I can't describe how that feels. You see somebody everyday, and you laugh and kid each other, and then you hear that he's dead, not from an accident, but shot, killed. I'd never been exposed to violence before, and now it surrounded me on all sides. I felt the world closing in, and my family was a thing of the past. It was as if one day I stopped being Marjorie Lindholm. Her life was gone, and this other girl's life was just a cheap imitation, but it's all there was.

Within a month or two, it was clear that the jeep had been an unwise purchase. It handled badly and had transmission problems. My father traded it in for my dream come true, a brand new sports car. Dreams can become nightmares. I saw my mother's heart break when she saw the car, and I didn't know what to do. Everybody thought I was a sell out, but at that point, I hadn't accepted the possibility that they were never going to get back together. I pictured us the way it was, and I'd have the car. I kept looking backward, because the road ahead was so ugly.

In the summer before my family split apart, I had a job at an ice cream shop just a few blocks from our house, again, straight down the street from Columbine. I was making minimum wage and probably ate more ice cream than I sold. A friend, Greg, also worked at that ice cream shop. He helped train me when I first started there. He was in my grade at Columbine, and we shared a couple of classes. He was very popular, a star basketball player.

Lots of girls had a crush on him; he worked hard and had a wonderful sense of humor. I can't say enough about him; he was just an all around great guy, but in the early part of May, 2000, I heard Greg hung himself. I remember telling my mom that I couldn't take anymore people I cared about dying; that it was ruining me, but I knew I had no control over that.

The world kept moving, and it's a violent place to be. Nobody is safe, and nowhere is safe. I don't remember anybody talking about how hard that was, not even me, but it was just so hard. I wondered if Greg hadn't known how much everyone liked him, and if he realized how many girls dreamed of going out with him, and if that ever would have mattered, but it didn't matter anymore.

He was gone, and I missed a step, and I fell a little farther behind.

Chapter 12
Learning To Cope With Impossible Choices

Soon, I moved back with my mother, while Sarah moved in with our father. The difference was day and night, and the choice was impossible. I lived a very comfortable lifestyle with my father. I drove a brand new car and wore expensive new clothes. My mother lived a very meager existence. People assumed that the money swayed the decision, and they made comments about it. I used to wonder if those same people ever even tried to consider all the things I had to consider. I loved them both, and my father had health problems. I used to wonder if other people ever thought about that, or if it was just easier to hear sound bites and pass judgment. It was mind bending and depressing.

My mother had no money, but around that time, she discovered that her aunt had left her a modest inheritance. It would be months before she received any of the proceeds, but it hung in the distance, the finish line. We believed that if we could make it through until the money was disbursed and the divorce was final, the hard times would be over.

My mother hadn't worked outside the home during their marriage, except for the work she did on the family businesses. We were living on borrowed funds and minimum wages in a neighborhood of expensive homes and new cars. It felt like we stuck out like a sore thumb. Some of David's friends called him poor, and it made my mother cry.

I started my senior year at Columbine already counting down the days to graduation. I dreaded going back. Everybody remembered the beautiful sports car, and now I had no vehicle. My father gave the car to Sarah to drive, after I moved back with my mother. The people at school remembered the beautiful clothes, and they were gone. I had signed up for a photography class when I was living with my father. It never occurred to me that I needed an expensive camera for that class. I never had to think about that type of thing while I lived with my father, but by the time school started, I was living with my mother. My father would only pay half, and my mother couldn't afford to pay even half of the camera's cost.

Columbine is a rich neighborhood. People divorce, but the lawyers work it out, and nobody ever really loses everything and ends up poor. That's how it felt, like we were a freak show or circus act that they wanted no part of. They were not going to take sides, and I was not going to receive special treatment. It seemed like I would buy the camera, or I would fail the class. It was all so embarrassing and shaming at the time; I couldn't take one more blow.

I stopped wanting to go to school; I stopped wanting to get up, and somehow my mother came up with her half of the money to buy the camera. I'll never forget that, and I just couldn't take it any more. I went to school with Sarah and David. Sarah lived the life of a rich girl, but was always nervous and upset. She cried all the time, but didn't want to leave our dad alone, while David qualified for the reduced price lunches. I stopped going, and I fell behind, and I didn't care.

But my mother cared. She suggested that I take the GED and enroll in college. I was a smart girl; maybe I just needed a change of scenery, and that's what I did. I took out student loans and enrolled in the state college, Spring Semester of 2001. Nobody knew I was from Columbine, and I never talked about it. Nobody knew my family's history, and I didn't have to explain it, and I loved it, and I started to catch up. I earned all A's and B's my first semester. I could see myself getting back on track. I could picture that.

My parent's divorce was final that June. My mother used borrowed money to hire a lawyer, while my father represented himself. He was very adept in and out of the courtroom.

My father maintained that he made no income other than his Veteran's Pension, and that he had no money. He claimed that all the possessions he had kept from my mother were worth next to nothing, and that the few pieces of jewelry she'd been wearing when she fled the house were worth thousands of dollars. He didn't budge an inch, as the clocked ticked, and my mother's legal fees mounted. The court ordered arbitration, and my father was to give my mother the car she drove, if she paid the hefty balance left on the loan secured by the car.

A few days before their final hearing, I was at my father's place. Just by chance, I happened across a copy of a cashier's check made out to my dad for a considerable amount of money. I thought it was a joke, a cruel hoax to dangle in front of my mother. I never dreamed it could be real, but it was. As it turned out, that money represented the proceeds of a lawsuit that had been going on for years between our family's business and some other Party. My mother had no idea it had settled, or that my father received the funds.

My mother's lawyer subpoenaed the bank cashier who cashed that check. She testified that she handed my father thousands of dollars in one hundred dollar bills within weeks of that hearing. None of the documents he filed with the court mentioned that money at all. When confronted with the facts and questioned about the whereabouts of the funds, my father claimed the money had vanished. He claimed that he thought I had stolen it. He really did that to me; my protector was gone. The judge awarded my mother ½ of that money, but the judge gave him months to pay it, and he never did. The judge never punished him for the accusations against me or for concealing the income from the court.

It broke my heart, but it was over. I wanted to move on and pick up the pieces. It seemed like things would be turning around for us, and my mother would be able to get back on her feet, until that evening. My father's friend and former business associate, Raymond, sued my mother. Raymond was a lawyer. My mother never saw that coming. She couldn't even understand the lawsuit, but she knew it would mean more attorneys' fees, and we were already struggling so much.

Within weeks after their final divorce decree, my father moved into a brand new house worth almost half a million dollars, just a few miles away from Columbine. My half sister, Joyce, owned that house. Sarah began driving a brand new convertible car, which was titled in Joyce's name.

Just two years before, we had been the epitome of family life, like what you would read about in a magazine. People looked up to us; people were jealous of us. Now our lives were closer to cartoon characters. One misfortune after another, yet we kept getting back up. Sometimes it felt like people liked seeing that. Maybe it was just my own bitterness, but that's how it felt, like some people thought we needed to be knocked down a peg, and I could feel it.

By then, I had gotten a job as a sales person for a wireless telephone company. I began to expand my horizons and make new friends. I started Fall Semester in college. The problem with falling behind is that you start to feel like you'll never catch up, and as soon as you start to make any progress, you begin to run, at least I do. I felt I couldn't move ahead quickly enough, and when my parent's divorce had finally ended, I may have let my guard down. When Raymond sued my mother, it hit me right between the eyes.

It seemed like outsiders were fueling the war between my father and my mother, that they were looting the family assets. It kept my mother in a constant state of poverty, thereby keeping me and my brother in poverty, and dooming Sarah to the impossible choice we had to make, and nobody cared.

My mom paid thousands of dollars in legal fees to defend herself against Raymond's claims. She borrowed that money against her upcoming inheritance, while Raymond represented himself. Eventually, she settled with Raymond for $1,000. Her attorney charged that much for one day in court, and she just wanted to move on. All the while, my father and Raymond continued to be friends. I've often wondered if Raymond did that as a favor for my dad. I prayed for justice, and I missed a step, and I fell behind, but nobody cared, except for my family.

A hard depression began to set in. It felt like I had lost my grounding. Nothing was safe or stable. I had always thought that my parents were an unbeatable team. So much of my self definition revolved around that truth, but that had crumbled. So many things I believed in had crumbled.

I started to feel like God's punching bag. I had to keep taking blow after blow of devastatingly hard stuff. I had to act strong, and look like I wasn't upset. I had to keep running to catch up, but it was burning me out. It was a crazy time.

My mother, David, and I had a tiny 2 bedroom apartment. The bedrooms were given to David and me, while my mom slept on the couch, a couch that my Aunt Joanne had given us. We owned nothing that somebody else hadn't owned before. It was hard, but we were managing.

After my mother paid thousands of dollars to pay off the car loan, my father did not sign the title over to her. Her attorney spent many hours seeking a Court Order. In the end, the Court signed the title, and my mother paid the attorney.

Somebody poured sugar in my mother's gas tank, and it had to be repaired. Then, somebody took out all 4 tires on her car with an ice pick, two different times. The damage was done in such a way that they could not be fixed, and she had to buy all new tires, twice. The police couldn't do anything, because there was no real evidence, only suspicions. The perpetrator was never apprehended. My mother spent more money and rented a garage. Thankfully, the vandalism stopped.

It was all but impossible not to feel like a victim all the time. We had no money, but the costs kept mounting. It all seemed so public at a moment when I craved privacy. It made me angry at the world, like the world let me down. I was just a cog in a wheel. The world kept moving, and people kept laughing, while my life fell apart. I missed my old self. I missed our old lives. I'd lay awake at night trying to figure everything out, but there was never any answer.

It's so hard to accept that you have no real control over the things that matter most in life. At least that's hard for me. We had no control over finances. We would scrimp and save pennies, only to have one act of vandalism cost more than we all made in a week. Things like that happened over and over, and it made me feel powerless and small. I couldn't find the answers within myself, so I looked outward. I tried to fill every moment of my time with some type of activity, so that I didn't have the opportunity to dwell on things I couldn't change.

Chapter 13
New Life /Old Memories

In September of 2001, I met a man, Hal. He worked with me, and there was an instant connection. I fell madly in love with him. I thought it was so romantic, and I wanted romance and flowers in my life. I wanted to feel the rush of happiness, and be a beautiful bride from a fairy tale.

Many people were quick to tell me it was a mistake, but those were the bean counters, the people who kept track of every step I had missed and every inch I had fallen behind. Those were the people who make judgments based on their tiny sound bites of information, and don't want to hear the details. I didn't listen; I didn't want to. The bean counters offered no real help or advice, just judgment and gossip.

Hal and I each got a tattoo on our back with the other's name, commitment tattoos to prove our love. I found myself celebrating the moment, and I held onto that feeling. I wanted to erase the tragic life I'd been leading and embrace a wonderful future, so after just six weeks, we were married.

Hal was quite a bit older than me, but he loved all the things I did. We'd go to the movies early on a Saturday and watch the latest flick, while we ate popcorn and candy. Then we'd sneak into a second movie after the first. There were times we actually snuck into a third movie, almost daring them to catch us. It was so much fun. We went to Mexico on our honeymoon and spent days on the beach. He tried to fill our time with excitement and romance, and when it was good, it was wonderful.

The whirlwind romance reeked havoc on my college classes, but I managed to maintain a respectable GPA. Hal's income was too high for me to qualify for financial aid, and I took bigger loans to pay for Spring Semester in college. My mother loved Hal like a son. David and Sarah loved him, and Hal and my father got along famously. In so many ways, it all seemed so perfect, but almost immediately, there were cracks in the foundation. I started to think our marriage was a mistake.

Love isn't always enough. I was barely nineteen years old. I had never lived away from my family. Hal was an exciting guy, but when the excitement died down, I was still me. That's probably the first time I realized that I just wasn't a happy person anymore, and I think Hal realized that too.

I found myself calling Brad more and more. I don't know why, maybe because he isn't really the happiest of people either. I don't have to smile when I see Brad; we aren't like that. It was probably clear that I had issues. Hal began to ask for details about my experience at Columbine. He wanted to help me through that, but I didn't think anybody could help. I didn't want to share that with him. I never shared those memories with anyone, not even myself. I despised those memories, and I did my best to stifle them.

I found myself depressed and sullen without reason, and I tried to hide that. In the short time we had known each other, he'd only seen me in a blissful state. It wasn't long before my old demons began to show up. The idea that he had fallen in love with that happy person made me insecure, and it fueled my depression.

Shades of Gray, that's what I call depression. It's one of the hardest things for me to deal with. I used to think that everything was black and white, good or bad, intentional or unintentional. I thought in a straight line, everything was mathematics. I could predict the outcome of anything by adding my actions with the logical reactions of the world. Now I just think that's a fairy tale, a fable parents tell their children to help them sleep at night.

Sometimes I think there's this whole huge gray area, a place where most of us live at least part of the time, and that scares me. When you enter the gray world, it's gradual, just a little bit darker than before, but a person has to be careful, because the shades of gray progressively become darker, so dark that you can lose all perspective. For the most part, there is no line in the sand. People sometimes can't see when they've crossed it, and too often, they can't see when other people are approaching it, so they can't stop them. People can do horrible things, and one bad act can be a ripple in the water, setting off a chain reaction that would never have occurred otherwise. Planning and working your whole life can't protect you from one outrageous act of another human being.

That thought is mind boggling and exhausting to me. There is no language of math in the real world. Math is absolute, you can count on it. Two plus two always equals four. For every action there is always an equal and opposite reaction; that's how it's supposed to be. When I was younger, that's how I thought it would be, but it's not, and it's not that way for anybody. Sometimes I feel like it's me, like I'm the only one who didn't know that, and I'm making a huge deal out of a simple fact of life. Everybody else has to deal with this stuff, whether they know it or not.

There is no red carpet for anybody. Maybe that's why it was so hard to seek help. I saw other people moving, living their lives, and dealing with the same problems I had. There are children who grow up in war zones, and others who grow up in famine. I'd seen it before, but it never seemed real, not the way it does now, and now I hurt for them. I hurt for everyone, and I'm angry that I'm not a stronger person.

Hal tried everything he could, events and distractions. That's what our marriage became. We took vacations and made wonderful memories. Hal bought me two tiny dogs, Belle and Ariel. They were a joy, but it wasn't enough. Looking back, it wouldn't have worked with anyone, not even the perfect man, and Hal was just like everyone else. He had issues of his own.

Maybe he thought that had he been a better husband, I would have been a happier bride. I don't know; we never talked about it. We talked about things that had no basis in reality, and I think I preferred that to addressing my real problems. I didn't want to talk about them.

Hal questioned my feelings about Brad. I felt like I had to keep looking for ways to prove my love to Hal. He wanted details about my experience at Columbine in order for us to share the same link I shared with Brad. I wouldn't do that; I'm not even sure why, but I drew a line in the sand.

I think it made him jealous of Brad, the fact that I shared something so riveting with another man, as if the memories of Columbine created a bond that undermined our marriage vows. In retrospect, I see the problem, but the solution still escapes me. In a perfect world, my husband would have been my best male friend, but the world is far from perfect, and for whatever reason, my best friend was Brad, and he was a guy. It all seemed so hopeless. I loved Hal, and I wanted our marriage to work, so I severed all ties with Brad. I lost the only friend who knew how I felt and didn't judge me. I lost my connection to the old me.

Chapter 14
Losing Touch/Losing Hope

During that semester, there was an incident. It was nothing, but it threw me off track. I remember sitting in Nutrition Class, trying to focus. Each classroom had a large white screen attached to the wall. The teacher would unroll the screen to show a video or movie. When not in use, it rolled neatly back into place. The professor in the room next to us was preparing to show a video, and he pulled down the screen. Inside my classroom, it sounded like a series of pops in quick succession, and it startled me. I started to freak out, and nobody in the room had any idea why. I was sobbing and couldn't stop shaking. I felt like I had to explain myself, and I did. I mentioned Columbine.

The room went silent, and I felt the eyes of the world on me. Somebody asked if the little pops made by the screen were what it sounded like that day, and I froze. I ran out of the room, and I went home. When I told Hal, he pressed me for details of my experience at Columbine. I totally shut down, and I shut him out.

I wanted to run to Brad, to sit in his living room, and tell him what happened with the screen. I wouldn't have to explain why I reacted so badly; he wouldn't even have asked. He wouldn't have asked details of the noise or anything else. I could picture us sitting, and knowing, and talking about sports or the weather. We were only friends, but I promised I'd never see him, and I didn't. I was alone, and I blamed Hal.

I began to have terrible nightmares. I tried to go back to school, but I never made it past the parking lot, and I failed every course. I forced myself to enroll the next semester. Looking back, that was probably a mistake, but I felt like I had to keep moving.

The world wasn't stopping, and I kept messing up. I took out more student loans, intent on catching up and getting a hold of myself. I got panicky and edgy when I walked back onto the campus. I thought if I could block the images of Columbine in my head, I would have it conquered, but the feelings started showing up.

I had a stomach ache that never went away. I was cold all the time, even when other people were fanning themselves and talking about the heat. I started to hear ringing in my ears, and at first, I asked people if they heard it, but when I realized they didn't, I knew it was just me. I was always looking around, expecting something. Sitting in a classroom was hell; I couldn't concentrate. I always had to sit by a door and find an exit route as soon as I entered the room. I didn't do well. I just couldn't go. As soon as I woke up, I'd be sick to my stomach.

It was like a barrier I couldn't cross, and I failed every class. I couldn't sit there anymore. Sometimes, I'd make it into the classroom, and leave within minutes. Sometimes, I only made it to the parking lot, and sometimes I didn't even try. By the end of that semester I owed almost $12,000 in student loans, had a GPA of 1.1, and was nowhere near a degree.

I felt myself falling farther and farther behind and losing hope. My mother urged me to get help, to see a doctor, and I did. The doctor prescribed the anti-depressant Lexipro. I began to feel better. I took out more student loans, and enrolled in college the following semester.

The depression lifted, and the constant upset cleared, but I couldn't muster the deep concentration needed to succeed in my courses. I wasn't depressed and crying every day. I decided the trade off between being able to focus on the minute was well worth the peace of mind the Lexipro provided. Although my coursework suffered, I was managing, but Lexipro was not covered by our insurance, and it became a drain on our finances. The doctor prescribed a different anti-depressant, but it was not the same. It offered little help for the cost of my concentration. It was no longer worth the trade off, and I stopped taking the medication.

About that time, my father began suing my mother. At one point, he had three different civil cases against her in District Court, in two different counties. He was simultaneously appealing their divorce decree, and he sued my mother's lawyer. He had stopped paying child support just months after the final orders of that court, and still hadn't paid any of the judgment. My mother's attorney's fees mounted into the tens of thousands of dollars. There was nothing left from her inheritance. Most of that money had been spent long before she ever received it.

Then, Joyce sued my mother. My mother's life was spent in courtrooms and lawyer's offices. Hearing after hearing, meeting after meeting, all for the price of her peace of mind and every dime she could ever hope to earn. I was watching the two people I loved most in the world battle each other on a daily basis, and I blamed myself. My mother spent many more thousands of dollars on attorneys before those cases were dismissed.

I'd lost my family so quickly. It seemed like we became different people in an instant, and it all started with Columbine. It seemed like those closest to my dad were encouraging the change. My mother was always stressed and upset. There was no money and nothing to show for it. There was nobody there to back us up. I felt like I'd lost everything.

It gets so old, fighting the world, trying to make things slow down, so that I could catch up. I loved my father; I still do, but I hated all the lawsuits. They drained so much money before each was dismissed. I hated watching my mother struggle to pay her rent, to put food on the table.

I remembered my life before Columbine, and I missed it. I wanted it back, but there was no going back. Once in motion, it just got bigger and bigger, like a ripple in the water. It touched everything and everyone, and it destroyed my once happy family. It destroyed my peace of mind.

I never knew life was so hard. I thought that schools were safe, and violence was not the norm. I thought the good guys always won, and that the courts protected regular people, but its not true, and I don't have an answer, but the world keeps moving, and that's just how it is. Maybe everyone else in the world knew that, but I never did.

It turned me to God. I wish I had some incredible words to resonate right now, but I'm just one person, one person who turned to God in desperation. Now, I pray all the time, for everyone, because the world scares me these days. I need God.

I failed college semester after semester. My marriage ended in the summer of 2003, and we went our separate ways. I moved back in with my mother. There were no I told you so's, or hoops to jump through. She welcomed me back, and David welcomed me back, and Sarah, who had moved home with my mother, welcomed me back. I realized that I was so far behind, that I might never catch up, but everyone was glad to see me. They were my backup, and they didn't judge.

It made me think that I hadn't lost everything, and life could go on. I went to see Brad. There are all different relationships throughout a person's life, and I don't know how to explain that one. He's not my boyfriend. There is nothing romantic, but we have a connection, and it's real. I can tell him a feeling or an event, and he doesn't judge, and he doesn't preach. He knows, and it means the world to me. Brad keeps in touch with a lot of us Columbine Survivors. He makes me feel like I'm not the only one. Now I believe that there may be a lot of us who can't sit in a classroom or deal with violence, and that my family was not the only one to break apart in its aftermath, but he has never named names, and I so respect that.

The last semester I went to school was spring of 2004, right after my divorce was final. I thought I could do it, but I couldn't. I refused to accept that fact until after the deadline to drop or change classes. By the time I sought help from my teachers and counselor, they couldn't do anything for me. It's not like people haven't tried; they really have, but it was almost like I was fighting the help they offered, like the only help I could allow would have to be on my own terms, and I refused to even discuss my feelings or the events that initiated the change in me. I accepted that it was hopeless.

My classes were on campus. I could have taken online courses, but not all degrees are available online. We didn't have internet or a decent computer at home. It was a very hard time, and I refused to allow myself space to recover, so I messed up again. Looking back, I could have done things differently, but there is a reason they say hind sight is 20/20.

I've tried a variety of occupations. I actually modeled quite a bit, but that is a true profession. I'm not sure if most people realize that. It looks easy, and it seems like the hardest part would be getting a job, any job. It only makes sense that a working model would make a good living. That's not always the case.

Models work very hard, and often go on several different interviews before finding out if they are hired. The work can be long, hard hours in high heeled shoes and hot bright lights. Models usually start much younger than I did, but it is exciting, and it was a great distraction from everyday life.

At one point, my picture was on a billboard for a new shopping mall. That same picture showed up in a national magazine advertisement. I used to think people got paid huge sums of money for something like that, but I didn't. I think I got about $500 for the photo shoot. The photographer owned the rights to the picture and must have sold it to various advertisers. It was a compliment, but it just didn't pay the bills.

I've worked as a waitress in various upscale restaurants and nightclubs. It's hard work, but I liked it, and I was just starting to think I'd found my niche. A few months ago, I had an incident, the latest in a string of triggers setting off my issues. I was working as a waitress at a local nightclub. I'd been there for about four months. The tips were great, and I loved my co-workers. Then there was a shooting outside. I heard huge gun fire and saw everyone running. We waited inside for an hour, while paramedics tried to resuscitate the victim, and detectives examined the scene.

I walked by the little numbers the police placed next to the evidence and the person's shirt stained in blood. I felt my mind begin to race, and then it went blank. I quit my job, on the spot. Everyone else seemed perfectly fine, scared, but not like me. Now I'm too nervous for that type of work.

Chapter 15
Self Appraisal and Starting Again

I'm realistic. For me, college is the surest way to success, the straightest line to financial security and self sufficiency. The world may not speak in the language of math, and there are no absolutes, but it does speak in the language of probability, and just like everyone else, I need to set my course based on those probabilities.

Right now, I think I have 25 credits I can use, and that's ridiculous, because I've gone to college for 3 years. I blame myself, but I can't seem to get it in gear. It's not the work; sitting there is insanely hard.

I still have nightmares, but they are different from regular nightmares, because it is so real in my head that I can picture myself or people around me in violent situations. I've seen dead bodies and puddles of blood. I've felt my life could end at any moment, and I relive that almost nightly. Those dreams leave me with little traumas that never happened. The dreams are so real, playing around in my head, leaving images that terrify me. I know they're not real, and I tell myself they aren't real, but it's distracting. I believe I should be stronger, and it's a disappointment. I disappoint myself.

I'm always amazed that people think there are special resources for people like me. Everybody seems to think that the fundraisers and donations after the

Columbine Tragedy provided the survivors with some type of benefit or financial help. They didn't. I got a few counseling sessions, but the time to get free counseling has long since expired. Back when it was available, I wasn't ready to talk. They built an expensive, beautiful library at the school, but I'll never use it. You couldn't pay me to use it.

This thing is like a wrecking ball waiting in the wings, just out of sight. It sits and waits for me to calm down and begin anew. Then it jumps on the first opportunity that arises, just to derail my plans. It stands in the way of college, and keeping a job, and living my life.

People see me and say that I'm cold, that I run away when they get too close. I'm sure that's how it looks, but there is a deeper truth, one that lies beneath the surface, where only those closest to me can see. I have a connection, a link to something dark and tragic. I can't share it with anyone, because I can't bear that it be exploited and turned into a flippant sound bite or some cheap video game in somebody's head.

Sometimes I feel like Columbine is my roommate, an uninvited guest that moved in without warning and will not leave no matter what I do. It shows up on holidays and family reunions. It changed who I was and who I became. It changed every day since that chilly Tuesday morning in April of 1999.

I feel like I lost everything to Columbine. I lost my security, peace of mind, and my dreams. I lost my family. To this day, I believe that Columbine was the trigger that set off my family's journey from synchronicity to the people that we became. It took everything, and still it won't leave.

I'm not saying that it didn't make me a stronger person, but when I was a little girl, I had a picture of myself, a vision of who I was to become. In those childhood dreams, all I had to do was work hard, and life was there for the taking. I could do anything, because nothing could stop me. I saw discouraged people and assumed that somehow their own actions had produced the result. Everyone had a sad story, but I justified that how you handled the situation determined your outcome. I was different; I made pink lemonade.

I know now that the pictures you see in newspapers and magazines are real. The interesting sound bites and news bits that you hear a hundred times a day are people's lives. They live in the aftermath of their personal tragedies long after interest has died down, long after it is newsworthy.

When I see the picture of a mother holding her dying child as she cries up to the heavens, I know that she can't imagine how life can go on, how people can still laugh and go out to lunch while her heart bleeds. It seems like the world should stand still, at least for a minute or two, out of respect, to help you catch your breath, but it doesn't. It keeps moving, and the longer it takes for you to move with it, the farther behind you fall, and the longer it will take you to catch up. I never knew that, until that day.

As I sit here today, I understand heartache, because I have experienced loss. I try not to judge, because I don't want to be judged. I realize that there are some things I still can't do, because even a fast moving freight train can be derailed, and getting back on track is all but impossible. Sometimes, I admire the person I have become, but I'd be lying if I told you that it's the person I set out to be, and I just can't stomach the taste of lemonade.

I hadn't seen my dad for a very long time. I guess there are still hurt feelings and raw nerves. He broke my heart. Then I saw him just last week. There were no apologies, and I wouldn't have believed an excuse, even if he offered one. I don't know if I can ever forgive him; I'm not sure if I have that much forgiveness in me.

Sarah is a college student and works almost full time. She has her own place and two little cats. We're not twins anymore, but we're still very close.

David and I have become the best of friends. He's really not my little brother anymore. He's over six feet tall. Every week we go to a local restaurant called Buffalo Wild Wings. We order buffalo wings and talk about the world. I must have been in a daze for way too long, because somewhere along the way, David became a man.

He already has his Associate's Degree and is seeking a Bachelor's. He even has plans for a Master's. He has no problem sitting in a classroom. In fact, he plans to be a college professor. I'm always teasing him that, if he keeps going at the rate he's going, I'll be a student in one of his classes, because I'm not much further than I was five years ago.

One of the wonderful things about David and Sarah is that they look up to me. I'm still important to them, and I can always go home. I hate to admit that, because I'm still the same person who believes no good can come from a tragedy, but Columbine taught me that. No matter who I am, there are people in this world who are glad to see me. It's amazing.

I still have my family, for the most part. To be honest, I don't consider my father a part of it. I can't change the past, and I can't forget all the unnecessary hardships we endured, no matter how much I wish I could. I live with my mother, and we're the best of friends. She works nights, and I work days, so we have to schedule our time together, but we're close.

My family thinks the best of me, at least those that matter. I don't believe that will ever change, but I still can't figure it out. Having my family is a gift, and I must be thankful. I'd be lying if I said I didn't miss the people we were, but I love how strong we've become, and I've learned so very much.

With all that, I still have problems. I need to get back on track. There doesn't seem to be many resources out there to help fix this. I know I need to pull myself together; I know I need to talk. That's a start. My mother is a Group Counselor these days. She's as good as they get. People nickname her groups "Standing Room Only" because everyone wants to be a part of it. Sometimes that means there aren't enough chairs, and they have to pull them in from other rooms.

My Aunt Theresa wrote a book after her mother died titled <u>Not Your Average Princess</u> by Theresa Keily Regenold. She and my mother had a very difficult childhood, and she considers herself a success story. I've read it, and I loved it. I realized I never knew her at all. She doesn't have any daughters, and people who know the both of us think I'm more like her than my own mother. Even I see that, and that's okay. There is a certain consolation in the fact that she didn't get her life together until long after she was my age. It gives me hope; she's actually a very happy person and has been for as long as I can remember.

My mother and Aunt Theresa meet most mornings to walk the lake and have a soda. When I have time, we're a trio, and I confessed my shortcomings one morning over a hot cup of tea in Target's café. The world didn't stop, and these two strong women didn't miss a beat.

I talked, and they listened, and I saw possibilities. My mother says that people need skills. She takes a piece of paper and draws two sides of a problem. On the left side, she labels the column "Stressors". On the right side are the words "Stress Relievers". Stressors are things that stress you out, triggers for negative thinking and behavior. Stress relievers are the skills a person uses to deal with the stressors.

She says that a person needs more stress relievers than the number of stressors they can list. Many people don't have positive stress relievers to cope with stress, but they can be learned, and it is just like gymnastics or schoolwork. The more you practice skills to relieve stress, the easier it is. That's exactly what she teaches in her groups.

She says that your mind is like a sponge or a computer. It can only hold so much, and that we can choose the data it stores. Sometimes, we just want to wring out the sponge or erase the hard drive and start over, but then we lose the good along with the bad. The trick is to diffuse the bad memories, to take away their power, and to stop using negative skills to cope with the stressors. When life gives you lemons, you can either carry them around while they get old and moldy and ruin everything they touch, or you can make lemonade. That's what it means, and I'm starting to get it.

My Aunt Theresa says that writing her book was a freeing experience. It gave her closure. As she wrote the final words, she closed the door on the past. Not from embarrassment or shame, but because it was time to move on. Her memories aren't buried, just put away for safe keeping. I like that idea. It made me think.

I'm working with my mother and my aunt. Learning from my mother and recording the journey. You're my group counseling session. I've told you things that I have never told another soul, not even Brad. I'm writing it down and saying it once, so I never have to explain it again. I'm writing down the good times too, the ones when I was little, and life was easy, so I don't forget them.

I'm starting again. I've enrolled in college and I have written this book with my mother. This time, all my classes will be online, because I think I can handle that. I believe in myself, but I'm not going to start running too soon. The world doesn't stop, but I'm not on anybody else's schedule. That's one of the skills my mother taught me. Sarah and David may graduate long before me, but it doesn't change who I am. I'm still the big sister, and they'll always think of me that way.

Even now it's hard, because the negative side of me says it's like I'm just setting myself up for failure. I owe about $20,000 in student loans, and it's hard not to focus on the financial hole I dug for myself, because I have no degree, but if I don't keep trying, the credits I've already earned are a waste.

When I really think about it, it's like I'm acting like I can do this, when I have no idea how I'm going to do this, but the world isn't stopping, and I need to get on board. Already I see growth, because as I write that, I realize how counterproductive those thoughts are. When they're swirling in my mind, they don't seem that way. They seem realistic, but reading them on paper is a whole different story. I need to keep writing; it gives me perspective.

For the first time in my life, I faced the worst day that ever happened to me, read it over and over again, and I'm still here. I didn't melt. My mother didn't melt, and my Aunt Theresa took our work and published it. I've come a long way; it's a process.

I'm not a freight train. I guess I never was. A freight train can't cry or hug its mom. A freight train can't chart its own course, and it will never know heartache. So I guess I'm not a freight train. I'm a Survivor...And a daughter, a sister, a friend, a cousin, a niece, a college student, and an author.

Thanks for listening.

ABOUT THE AUTHORS:

Peggy Lindholm is a Licensed Professional Counselor practicing in Denver, Colorado and the surrounding area.

She specializes in seminars and group counseling sessions designed to increase her clients':

- Self-Esteem
- Anger Management Skills
- Life Skills

For more information,

Visit her website at: WWW.PEGZGROUPS.COM

Marjorie Lindholm is a twenty-two year old college student attending Arapahoe Community College through their online internet classes. She is currently working on her Associates Degree.

You may contact Marjorie through Regenold Publishing at:

www.regenoldpublishing.com

Regenold Publishing
PO Box 621967
Littleton, CO 80162-1967

ORDER INFORMATION

A Columbine Survivor's Story

Is available for $12.99 each with free shipping.

For fastest service or credit card payment,
ORDER ONLINE:

www.regenoldpublishing.com

Or use this order form:

QTY	Unit Price	Sub-Total (qty x 12.99)	Colo Residents Add 4.6% Tax	Amount Enclosed
	12.99			

Name:
Address:
Email:

Colorado Residents add 4.6% sales tax.

Make check or money order payable to:

Regenold Publishing Co.
PO Box 621967
Littleton, CO 80162-1967